WORDS
TO
INSPIRE
EVERYDAY
LIVING

COMPILED BY SARAH HOGGETT

DESIGN BY DAVID FORDHAM

CICO BOOKS

LONDON NEW YORK

First published in 2007 by CICO BOOKS
An imprint of
Ryland Peters & Small
20–21 Jockey's Fields   519 Broadway, 5th Floor
London WC1R 4BW   New York, NY 10012

10 9 8 7 6 5 4 3 2 1

A CIP catalog record for this book is available from the Library of Congress
and the British Library.

US ISBN-13: 978 1 904991 71 7
US ISBN-10: 1 904991 71 8

UK ISBN-13: 978 1 904991 70 0
UK ISBN-10: 1 904991 70 X

Printed in China

Designer: David Fordham

LIFE
&
INSPIRATION

WORDS
TO
INSPIRE
EVERYDAY LIVING

CONTENTS

LIFE

&

INSPIRATION

INTRODUCTION

There are times in all our lives when we hear someone say something so simple, yet so obviously full of truth, that it's as if a light bulb has suddenly been switched on in our mind, illuminating the way forward. There are times when we want to offer encouragement to our loved ones, but find it difficult to find the right words. And there are times when a quirky quip that makes someone laugh through their tears is a better medicine than any doctor could prescribe.

WORDS FOR EVERYDAY INSPIRATION is a compilation of memorable quotations from the great and the good, the wise and the witty. Within its pages you will find words of wisdom from ancient philosophers, uplifting thoughts from poets and politicians, and phrases that may just make you stop and think for a moment about your attitude to life and the direction in which you're heading.

There are all kinds of ways in which you can use the quotations. Inscribe them in homemade greetings cards or on a scrapbook layout commemorating a special occasion. Pin your favorites to your office notice board, where they will serve as a daily reminder to live your life to the full and to the best of your ability. Text or e-mail them to your friends and family. Or simply dip into this book from time to time and take inspiration from what you find.

And remember: in the words of Grandma Moses,

" LIFE IS WHAT WE MAKE IT, *ALWAYS* HAS BEEN, *ALWAYS* WILL BE. "

"YOU CANNOT OPEN A BOOK WITHOUT LEARNING SOMETHING."

Confucius (551–479 BCE)

THE POWER
OF
LAUGHTER

"A GOOD LAUGH IS SUNSHINE IN THE HOUSE."

William Makepeace Thackeray (1811–1863)

"IT TAKES 25 MUSCLES TO
SMILE,
AND 62 MUSCLES TO
FROWN."

Anon

"THE HUMAN RACE HAS ONE
REALLY EFFECTIVE WEAPON, AND
THAT IS LAUGHTER."

Mark Twain (1835–1910)

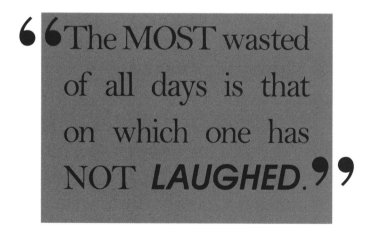

"The MOST wasted
of all days is that
on which one has
NOT *LAUGHED*."

Nicolas Chamfort (1741–1794)

"What SUNSHINE is to flowers, SMILES are to humanity."

Joseph Addison (1672–1719)

"One *joy* scatters a hundred *griefs*."

Chinese proverb

13

"LAUGH, AND THE WORLD LAUGHS WITH YOU; WEEP, AND YOU WEEP ALONE."

Ella Wheeler Wilcox (1850–1919)

"LAUGH AND THE WORLD LAUGHS WITH YOU, SNORE AND YOU SLEEP ALONE."

Anthony Burgess (1917–1993)

"There are three
things which are real:
**GOD, HUMAN FOLLY,
& LAUGHTER.**
The first two
are beyond our
comprehension. So we
must do what we can
with the third."

John F. Kennedy (1917–1963)

QUOTES
&
QUIPS
FOR POSITIVE
THINKING

"WHEREVER YOU **GO**, **GO** WITH ALL YOUR HEART."

Confucius (551–479 BCE)

"DO NOT DWELL IN THE PAST, DO NOT DREAM OF THE FUTURE, CONCENTRATE THE MIND ON THE PRESENT MOMENT."

Buddha (563–483 BCE)

66 YOU CAN DO ANYTHING IF
YOU HAVE ENTHUSIASM.
ENTHUSIASM IS THE YEAST
THAT MAKES YOUR HOPES
RISE TO THE STARS. WITH IT,
THERE IS ACCOMPLISHMENT.
WITHOUT IT THERE ARE ONLY
ALIBIS. 99

Henry Ford (1863–1947)

"As to me,
I know of
nothing
else but
miracles."

Walt Whitman (1819–1892)

"A TOWER OF NINE STOREYS BEGINS WITH A HEAP OF EARTH.

THE JOURNEY OF A THOUSAND *LI* STARTS FROM WHERE ONE STANDS."

Lao Tzu (*c.* 604–531 BCE)

STOREYS
STOREYS
STOREYS
STOREYS
STOREYS
STOREYS
STOREYS
STOREYS
STOREYS
STOREYS

"KEEP YOUR EYES ON THE STARS

Theodore Roosevelt (1858–1919)

AND YOUR FEET ON THE GROUND."

WHEN LIFE SEEMS HARD

" I've learned that no matter what happens, or how bad it seems TODAY, life does go on, and it will be better TOMORROW. "

Maya Angelou (1928–)

"WHEN YOU GET
TO THE END
OF YOUR ROPE,
TIE A KNOT
AND

H
A
N
G
ON."

Franklin D. Roosevelt (1882–1945)

"NOTHING IS PARTICULARLY HARD IF YOU DIVIDE IT INTO SMALL JOBS."

Henry Ford (1863–1947)

"IF *WINTER* COMES, CAN *SPRING* BE FAR BEHIND?"

Percy Bysshe Shelley (1792–1822), 'Ode to the West Wind'

" WHEN YOU GET INTO A TIGHT PLACE AND EVERYTHING GOES AGAINST YOU TILL IT SEEMS YOU COULD NOT HOLD ON A MINUTE LONGER, NEVER GIVE UP THEN FOR THAT IS JUST THE PLACE AND TIME THAT THE TIDE WILL TURN. "

Harriet Beecher Stowe (1811–1896)

"A WOMAN IS LIKE
A TEABAG. IT'S ONLY
**WHEN SHE'S IN
HOT WATER THAT
YOU REALIZE HOW
STRONG SHE IS."**

Nancy Reagan (1921–)

"HOWEVER LONG THE N I G H T, THE D A Y WILL BREAK."

African proverb

"AFTER ALL, TOMORROW IS ANOTHER DAY."

Margaret Mitchell (1900–1949)

"YOU GAIN
STRENGTH, COURAGE, &
CONFIDENCE
BY EVERY EXPERIENCE IN
WHICH YOU REALLY STOP TO
LOOK FEAR IN THE FACE."

Eleanor Roosevelt (1884–1962)

" *REFLECT* ON YOUR PRESENT **BLESSINGS,** OF WHICH EVERY MAN HAS MANY; *NOT* ON YOUR PAST **MISFORTUNES** OF WHICH ALL MEN HAVE SOME. "

Charles Dickens (1812–1870)

"THE LONGER
WE DWELL
ON OUR
MISFORTUNES,
THE GREATER
IS THEIR
POWER TO
HARM US."

Voltaire (1694–1778)

LIVE LIFE
TO
THE FULL

"Live **ALL** you can; it's a mistake not to. It doesn't so much matter what you do in particular, so long as you have your **LIFE**. If you haven't had that, what have you had?"

Henry James (1843–1916)

" MAY YOU LIVE EVERY DAY OF YOUR LIFE. "

Jonathan Swift (1667–1745)

"Twenty years from now you will be more disappointed by the things you didn't do than by the ones you did. So throw off the bowlines. Sail away from the safe harbor. Catch the trade winds in your sails. Explore. Dream."

Mark Twain (1835–1910)

"FAR AWAY THERE IN THE SUNSHINE ARE MY HIGHEST ASPIRATIONS. I MAY NOT REACH THEM, BUT I CAN LOOK UP AND SEE THEIR BEAUTY, BELIEVE IN THEM, AND TRY TO FOLLOW WHERE THEY LEAD."

Louisa May Alcott (1832–1888)

" IRON RUSTS FROM DISUSE;

STAGNANT WATER LOSES
ITS PURITY AND IN COLD
WEATHER BECOMES FROZEN;

Leonardo da Vinci (1452–1519)

EVEN SO
DOES INACTION SAP THE
VIGOUR OF THE MIND. "

"WE SHOULD NOT LET OUR FEARS HOLD US BACK

FROM *PURSUING* OUR HOPES."

John F. Kennedy (1917–1963)

" Dream no SMALL dreams for they have no power to move the hearts of men. "

Johann Wolfgang von Goethe (1749–1832)

" OPPORTUNITY IS MISSED BY MOST PEOPLE BECAUSE IT IS DRESSED IN OVERALLS AND LOOKS LIKE WORK. "

Thomas Edison (1847–1931)

"No bird SOARS too HIGH if he SOARS with his own wings."

William Blake (1757–1827)

MAKE THE WORLD A BETTER PLACE

"IT IS THE GREATEST OF ALL MISTAKES TO DO NOTHING BECAUSE YOU CAN ONLY DO A LITTLE. DO WHAT YOU CAN."

Sydney Smith (1771–1845)

"WE OURSELVES FEEL THAT WHAT
WE ARE DOING IS JUST A

DROP
IN THE OCEAN. BUT IF THAT

DROP
WAS NOT IN THE OCEAN,
I THINK THE OCEAN WOULD
BE LESS BECAUSE OF THAT
MISSING DROP.
I DO NOT AGREE WITH THE

BIG

WAY OF DOING THINGS."

Mother Teresa of Calcutta (1910–1997)

" *TREAT THE EARTH WELL: IT WAS NOT GIVEN TO YOU BY YOUR PARENTS, IT WAS LOANED TO YOU BY YOUR CHILDREN.* "

Native American saying

46

" *Service to others is the rent you pay for your room here on earth.* "

Muhammad Ali (1942–)

"EACH TIME A MAN STANDS UP FOR AN IDEAL, OR ACTS TO IMPROVE THE LOT OF OTHERS, OR STRIKES OUT AGAINST INJUSTICE, HE SENDS FORTH A TINY RIPPLE OF HOPE, AND CROSSING EACH OTHER FROM A MILLION DIFFERENT CENTRES OF ENERGY AND DARING, THOSE RIPPLES BUILD A CURRENT THAT CAN SWEEP DOWN THE **MIGHTIEST** WALLS OF OPPRESSION AND RESISTANCE."

Robert F. Kennedy (1925–1968)

"To EASE another's heartache is to FORGET one's own."

Abraham Lincoln (1809–1865)

49

IF YOU WANT ONE YEAR OF PROSPERITY, GROW GRAIN. IF YOU WANT TEN YEARS OF PROSPERITY, GROW TREES. IF YOU WANT ONE HUNDRED YEARS OF PROSPERITY, GROW PEOPLE".

Chinese proverb

"'TIS NOT ENOUGH TO HELP THE FEEBLE UP,

William Shakespeare (1564–1616)

BUT TO SUPPORT HIM AFTER."

"If you have only one smile in you, give it to the people you love. Don't be surly at home, then go out in the street and start grinning **'Good morning'** at total strangers."

Maya Angelou (1928–)

"A SOCIETY GROWS GREAT WHEN OLD MEN PLANT TREES IN WHOSE SHADE THEY KNOW THEY SHALL NEVER SIT."

Greek proverb

**Do ALL THE GOOD YOU CAN,
BY ALL THE MEANS YOU CAN,
IN ALL THE WAYS YOU CAN,
IN ALL THE PLACES YOU CAN,
AT ALL THE TIMES YOU CAN,
TO ALL THE PEOPLE YOU CAN,
AS LONG AS EVER YOU CAN.**

John Wesley (1703–1791)

"WHAT DO WE LIVE FOR; IF IT IS NOT TO MAKE LIFE *LESS* DIFFICULT FOR EACH OTHER?"

George Eliot (1818–1890)

BELIEVE IN YOURSELF

"THIS ABOVE ALL; TO THINE OWN SELF BE TRUE."

William Shakespeare (1564–1616)

" WHEN YOU MEET SOMEONE
BETTER THAN YOURSELF, *TURN*
YOUR THOUGHTS TO BECOMING
HIS EQUAL.

Confucius (551–479 BCE)

WHEN YOU MEET SOMEONE
NOT AS GOOD AS YOU ARE,
LOOK WITHIN AND EXAMINE
YOUR OWN SELF. "

"I'M THE GREATEST!"

Muhammad Ali (1942–)

"WHEN YOU HAVE FAULTS, DO NOT FEAR TO ABANDON THEM."

Confucius (551–479 BC)

"GOD gave us the GIFT OF LIFE; it is up to us to give ourselves the GIFT OF LIVING WELL."

Voltaire (1694–1778)

"LOVE NOT WHAT YOU ARE, BUT WHAT YOU MAY BECOME."

Miguel de Cervantes (1547–1616)

66 KEEP AWAY FROM PEOPLE WHO TRY TO belittle YOUR AMBITIONS. SMALL PEOPLE ALWAYS DO THAT, BUT THE REALLY GREAT MAKE YOU FEEL THAT YOU, TOO, CAN BECOME GREAT. 99

Mark Twain (1835–1910)

"NOTHING
can bring you peace but yourself."

Ralph Waldo Emerson (1803–1882)

"*WHATEVER YOU ARE,*
be a
GOOD ONE."

Abraham Lincoln (1809–1865)

INDEX
of
AUTHORS

SOURCES AND ACKNOWLEDGMENTS

The publishers are grateful for permission to reproduce extracts from works in copyright.

p. 15 Anthony Burgess: From *The Complete Enderby* by Anthony Burgess, published by Vintage. Reproduced by permission of The Random House Group Ltd

p. 19 Henry Ford

p. 24 Maya Angelou: In conversation with Oprah Winfrey

p. 28 Nancy Reagan: From address given to US Women's Congress, quoted in the *Observer*, London, 29 March 1981

p. 26 Henry Ford

p. 45 Mother Teresa of Calcutta: From *A Gift for God*, reproduced by permission of HarperSanFrancisco

p. 47 Muhammad Ali: Quoted in *Time* magazine (1978)

p. 51 Maya Angelou: Extract from *Singin' and Swingin' and Gettin' Merry Like Christmas* © Maya Angelou 1976. Reproduced by permission of Virago Press, a division of Little, Brown Book Group

p. 58 Muhammad Ali: Quoted in *Louisville Times*, 26 November 1962

Every effort has been made to contact copyright holders and acknowledge sources, but the publishers would be glad to hear of any omissions.